Victory Over Every Appointment With Death

DELIVERANCE SERIES VOLUME 10

Bishop Climate Irungu

Bishop Climate Ministries
PO Box 67884
London, England SE5 9JJ
www.bishopclimate.org
Email: prayer@bishopclimate.org
Tel: +44 7984 115900 (UK)
Tel: +44 207 738 3668 (UK)
Tel: +732 444 8943 (USA)

Contents

Appointed to Death

For he hath looked down from the height of his sanctuary, from heaven did the LORD behold the earth, to hear the groaning of the prisoner, to loose those that are appointed to death.

(Psalms 102:19-20)

In the name of King Ahasuerus it was written, and sealed with the king's signet ring. And the letters were sent by couriers into all the king's provinces, to destroy, to kill, and to annihilate all the Jews, both young and old, little children and women, in one day, on the thirteenth day of the twelfth month, which is the month of Adar, and to plunder their possessions.

(Esther 3:12-13)

PART ONE

What are Demonic Appointments?

One day a lady came to see me at my office. She was doing her PHD at the University of Edinburgh. And she began to tell me about a man back home where she came from. He was a good man, many times repairing her car even when she didn't have any money. And she told me how one day he was convicted of murder. For the past 10 years he has been in jail and because there is a capital punishment in the country where they come from he was facing death row.

But she said, "Man of God, I know this man is innocent. And I believe that God can do something. Please help me". I remember hearing the pain in this woman's voice as she spoke. And I began asking God, "Lord, is there an answer for the people who have already been sentenced? Is there a way out for those people whose fate has already been sealed?" And God brought me to the scripture in Psalms 102:19-20,

> For he hath looked down from the height of his sanctuary; from heaven did the LORD behold the earth; to hear the groaning of the prisoner; to loose those that are appointed to death.

So I came into agreement with the lady as I shared with her the power of agreement and I prayed with her and loosed her friend from that appointed death. The next week she came to tell me that the man had been released from jail and all the charges against him had been dropped. He was now a free man!

Child of God, what am I trying to say here? There are some of you that, without knowing, have already been appointed to death. Just like the way you have an appointment to go to work or an appointment with the doctor, there is a demonic appointment that has already been set. You ask me what is an appointment? An appointment is when a meeting has been pre-arranged for a specific time or place.

When you have an appointment with death, it won't matter what you try to do to avoid it; after all is said and done you will end up facing that appointment. If you don't die from disease, it will be by car accident; if it's not this, it will be that. One way or another you will never end up reaching old age because already your fate has been sealed where your life is concerned.

One day I heard a very sad story about a lady who travelled back to Uganda. She had been working in the UK for many years and had built up properties back home with the money she earned. When she was about to go home she had let some of her friends and family know that she was coming. When she got to Uganda and arrived at her house, she didn't know that a band of robbers had been hired to hit her. When she entered the house, they attacked her and smashed her body until it was flat. They completely destroyed her. Unfortunately that lady had an appointment with death; someone had already sentenced her that she would die a horrible death. But that is not your portion in the name of Jesus.

In the same way, when you have an appointment with singleness it won't matter how many relationships you try, they will all end up the same way. When you see people who have an appointment with sickness and disease, they are always jumping from one hospital to another hospital searching for a solution but never getting any better. But I'm here to tell you that that will no longer happen in Jesus name.

Some of you have been born into families where their fate has already been sealed. Somebody went and made a sacrifice and sentenced your family to death. They have already sealed it so that you will die a painful death. They have gone and sentenced your family to poverty and you find that no matter what you try, you end up suffering. You can work so hard, get rich, have a good life, but when you have been sentenced to poverty you will end up losing it all.

I've seen people fight so hard to maintain their marriages, their careers, etc. but they always end up in the same footsteps as their family. Many people often move from continent to continent in search of a better life only to find that things get even worse. Because when your family has been sealed or when your fate has been sealed there is nothing you can do about it. For some of you, your enemies have even named your family. When they talk about them they say, "The family that is doomed; the family where people never get married; the family of drunkards; the family of thieves; the family that is always selling their land; the family that never finishes anything". But today we bind every negative word and every idle tongue that has been raised against us in the name of Jesus.

God spoke to Abraham and said that for 400 years his children would be oppressed and treated as slaves. There was an appointment that was already set for them and no matter what they did they had to meet their appointment. Why? Because there are some situations in life where you find that once the appointment has been made there is no other option but to meet it. Some of the things that you're going through have nothing to do with you. That's why no matter how much you know or you try to do, you can't seem to get out of them. But it's because you don't know the root cause of it. What you didn't know is that you were born into that curse; you inherited it by birth. And the root to all the bad luck and tragedies you have been experiencing is spiritual. But the time to rise up is now. Praise God that today a higher power is about to intervene in your life and cancel every demonic appointment in the name of Jesus!

Today there are many born-again Christians walking on time bombs. Their fate has already been sealed; their destiny decided; their chapter closed. But how does this happen?

Read the following scripture very well,

For he hath looked down from the height of his sanctuary; from heaven did the LORD behold the earth; to hear the groaning of the prisoner; to loose those that are appointed to death.

(Psalms 102:19-20)

What it's talking about is someone that has already been appointed to die. It's not that they shall be appointed but that their fate has already been sealed. There is someone reading this book and I see that your fate has already been sealed. Whether you like it or not, it is just a matter of time before you face it. But I'm here to tell you, fear not! By you reading this book, your faith has been activated and as a result God is about to change your situation around in the name of Jesus.

PART TWO

Three Reasons Behind Demonic Appointments

1. Generational Curses

One of the main reasons where you will find yourself having a pre-appointed fate is as a result of generational curses. This is where you find reoccurring problems within the family. It is within the bloodline; within the DNA. Just like when you go to see a medical doctor for the first time and they ask you for your family medical history, in the same way you can evaluate your family's spiritual history by searching for any related issues.

When there is a generational curse over your family, that train of failure will stop at every generation and then keep moving. Things like marriage failure, singleness, sickness and disease, premature death, poverty, struggle, lust, madness, etc. You will find that for one reason or another there was a curse pronounced over your family's life and it is still affecting you. Sometimes it only affects the male side or vice versa. But today I declare: may the Lord purge away every generational hindrance you have been carrying in Jesus name. May the Lord cleanse your blood from every spiritual disease in the mighty name of Jesus.

> For I will cleanse their blood that I have not cleansed.
>
> (Joel 3:21)

2. Personal Mistakes/Sin

Another reason you may have a demonic appointment is because of things you have done personally in your own life. Many times, the problems that born-again Christians face are a result of things they have gone and done personally. There are some things you can do that can invoke curses over your life; things that will seal your fate. You may find that you have already appointed yourself to death. Especially once you are born again, it is important that you live right. It is one thing to do something without knowing but once you are in God and you have knowledge of the truth it is entirely different.

Don't ever go around breaking up people's marriages, mocking people, or mistreating the blind, elderly, and disabled. And especially things like abortion or terminating lives. You can't be a born again Christian and then go do those things. You have to live right; otherwise you are cursing yourself. Then who can you call on for help?

> If we deliberately keep on sinning after we have received the knowledge of the truth, no sacrifice for sins is left.
>
> (Hebrews 10:26)

I've seen born-again Christians going to witch doctors. Now what do you expect is going to happen? You have started your deliverance and then you go and visit a witch doctor. How is anything good going to come out of that? You can't go around cutting covenants with the devil and expect to succeed. There are some covenants you have gone and cut without knowing and now because you're not fulfilling them they have backfired on you. Now your finances are being destroyed, your marriage is falling to pieces and you are the one that put yourself in that situation. You have put yourself on death row. But I'm here to let you know that we serve a merciful God who is able to restore us. We serve a God who doesn't reward us according to our mistakes.

3. Witchcraft

The other reason for a demonic appointment in our lives is one of the most common, which comes from witchcraft, voodoo, or juju. This is where people bind you because of jealousy. And as a result they sentence your family to sickness; they sentence your family to poverty. Some people don't know how hard you have worked, they don't know you have been working multiple jobs but as soon as they see you building up a small house, jealousy rises up and witchcraft is released against you.

Many times, once they hear you have gone abroad, they go and make a demonic sacrifice and sentence you to poverty. It seems that people always want to be on top of one another. Even in your working place, you will find there is always a fight for power. Often times in government, when a family member is running for political power, the whole family will get destroyed because of jealousy. But today we are going to break that in Jesus name!

I want you to go and read the story of Esther from chapters 5-7. The Bible says that Mordecai and the entire family of Jews were appointed to death. But as Haman was preparing the gallows, the place where they would be slaughtered, that God caused the king to have no peace. And he woke up in the middle of the night and began to read the history books. Child of God I saw that God was pulling out a file and it had your name on it. I don't know who has set that appointment for you, I don't know who it is that has sealed your fate, but I'm here to let you know that

God has not forgotten you. Today God is reviewing your case in the name of Jesus.

I love the book of Esther because it reveals to us how the world of wickedness works. Haman sealed the fate of the Jews by issuing a decree of death. But not only that, he made it clear the specific date that they should die. It was an appointment.

> In the name of King Ahasuerus it was written, and sealed with the king's signet ring. And the letters were sent by couriers into all the king's provinces, to destroy, to kill, and to annihilate all the Jews, both young and old, little children and women, in one day, on the thirteenth *day* of the twelfth month, which *is* the month of Adar, and to plunder their possessions.
>
> (Esther 3:12-13)

Once a decree had been issued and sealed with the King's signet ring, it was irrevocable. Can you imagine what was going through the minds and hearts of the Jewish community; knowing that at a specific day and time they would all die, and that the people who killed them would be paid highly from the king's treasury?

Today I declare that every appointment with death in your life is cancelled in the Mighty Name of Jesus. You are going to live long! Yes I declare that you will out-live all your enemies in the name of Jesus!

Let me tell you something. I want you to know that you may not get the privilege to know who or when your appointment is but as a man of God the spirit of God has instructed me to help you just like he helped Mordecai. And I am going to help expose every plan of your enemies to eliminate you; to eliminate your career; your family; your marriage.

There is someone very spiritually powerful that has been appointed to terminate you. Somebody has paid some sums of money to eliminate you. I know what has been happening, but now you must rise up like Esther. You must seek a higher power.

Did you know a High court is greater than a Magistrate court? It is only a High court that can revoke what has been decided at the Magistrate court. In the same way, a creation is not greater than the Creator. Now satan and his cohorts are just a creation but me and you we can seek the higher power from the Creator and get that judgement revoked Amen!

And the Bible says that the king read the book of records all night long until he was consoled. Haman had worked so hard to ensure that Mordecai and the rest of the Jews met their appointment but God had another appointment planned for them.

I don't know who it is that has been working against you but I declare their plans shall no longer prevail in your life. Some of you have been marked for that demonic appointment but right now I declare that every mark that has been assigned by the enemy to identify you as a prisoner, to oppress you, to take away all your rights, to hinder your progress, today I declare let it die by fire!

Every spirit of jealousy that is unable to tolerate you, today we bind it in the name of Jesus. Enough is enough! Today every generational curse over your life is going to be broken. You are not going to go the way that everyone else has gone. You are not going to follow the same footsteps of your family but may the Lord begin to order your steps in the name of Jesus. For some of you, your family has been sentenced to death, sentenced to poverty, sentenced to sickness, but today I reject that in the name of Jesus.

Many of you have been trying so hard but it seems that something is always surrounding you and cutting off your blessing. Why? Because your fate is already sealed. But listen to me. The Bible says that we are sealed with the Holy Spirit so we are going to remove every demonic seal that has already sealed you, packed you, and destined you for destruction. We are going to break that seal in the name of Jesus.

If you have ever worked with customs, you would know what I'm talking about. When a container is about to be shipped out of a country, it must be packed, inspected, and then sealed. And once it is sealed, that seal cannot be removed until it arrives at its destination. And it is the same thing in the spirit.

For some of you, your family has been packed, sealed, and shipped to destruction. But today we are going to recall you back. We are going to remove that seal of destruction. We are going to remove that seal of poverty and replace it with the seal of prosperity. We are going to recall that seal of sickness. The days of you being in and out of hospital are over. The days of you going up and down are no more. After today, it will be up, up, up, up, up! I prophesy over your life, you will never come down in the name of Jesus. The days of struggle are over. And anyone who wants to put a new seal on your life, as they stretch their hands against you I declare may the Lord deal with them in the name of Jesus.

> For he hath looked down from the height of his sanctuary; from heaven did the Lord behold the earth; To hear the groaning of the prisoner; to loose those that are appointed to death;
>
> (Psalms 102:19-20)

I know that today the Lord will look from heaven and hear all your cries that you have been going through. Today every fate that has been sealed against your life must die by fire. If you know that you have been experiencing a circle of death in your family or business, if you have been losing jobs suddenly for no reason, then you need to get serious in prayer and visit our deliverance centre. Let this curse be broken out of your life once and for all.

As the Prophet of God over your life, please remember that you can contact me and we can arrange for your deliverance. I see every appointment with death in your life, marriage, business, health, family, and finances being cancelled in Jesus Name.

Today as you read this book and pray, the snare you have been in for years is going to be broken. You are about to experience peace like never before. You will be able to know the right direction you need to go in. For the first time, whatsoever you choose to do will succeed. And you are going to experience breakthrough and favour in Jesus name.

Destroy Every Appointment With Death

Before you pray, remember to put on the full armor of God according to Ephesians 6:10-18, touching each part of your body as you say it.

Repeat with me: "I put on the full armor of God. The helmet of salvation upon my head, the breastplate of righteousness in its place, the belt of truth around my waist, my feet shod with the readiness of the gospel of peace, taking the shield of faith in my left hand and the sword of the spirit in my right".

In the Name of Jesus:

1. I take authority against every ruler, against all authorities, against all powers of darkness and every spiritual-wickedness in high places. Satan the blood of Jesus is against you

2. In the name of Jesus I take authority and I cancel every demonic appointment with death, I dismantle it in Jesus name!

3. I cancel every appointment with death, with failure, with sickness, and with poverty in the name of Jesus!

4. I remove every demonic seal that has been placed upon me and my family in the name of Jesus!

5. Every pre-determined fate over my life I cancel it in the mighty name of Jesus!

6. Every demonic sentence to marriage failure, to parental failure, to financial failure, to bodily failure, I revoke it in the name of Jesus!

7. Any person who has been causing demonic appointments in my life through witchcraft let them die by fire!

8. Every spirit of death that has been chasing me I command it to by die by fire!

9. In the mighty name of Jesus I refute every demonic proclamation over my children and my future!

10. Every appointment with sickness die by fire in the name of Jesus!

11. Every appointment with tragedies die by fire in the name of Jesus!

12. Every appointment with spiritual and physical robbers die by fire in the name of Jesus!

13. Every appointment with chronic diseases and problems die by fire in the name of Jesus Christ!

14. Every appointment with shame and disgrace I cancel it and I command it to die by fire!

15. Every evil mark that has been put upon me that attracts death, that attracts failure, that attracts singleness, that attracts poverty, I destroy it in the mighty name of Jesus!

16. Every evil force that has risen against me to keep me in the same footsteps as my family, I plea the blood of Jesus against it now. I command it to die by fire!

17. I cancel every name they have called me and my family that has kept us in bondage in the name of Jesus!

18. Right now, I untie myself from every generational curse that has been following me in the name of Jesus!

19. I command every train that has been carrying destruction to stop for the last time in the name of Jesus!

CONCLUSION

What Can I Expect?

So now that you have your prayer points you need to understand that deliverance is not a onetime event but a process and you need to be consistent if you are going to destroy the enemies in your life. Let's look at a few things you can expect while going through your deliverance.

Firstly, expect to be set free and for peace to return back into your life. The Bible says that those who wait for the Lord shall not be ashamed. Also, start expecting God to give you a testimony, just like everyone else who has gone through our deliverance program.

There are some key steps you can follow to ensure you are doing everything properly in order to obtain your desired goals. (These are in addition to your daily prayer points listed in this book)

1. Locate the area of your need

According to what your situation may be, you need to identify the particular area, or areas, which are most dire.

2. Find out what the Word of God says regarding that area

Select the appropriate scriptures promising you what you desire and meditate upon them. Write them on your walls where you can see them. Even if it means writing it on yourself so you won't forget to recite them during the day. Do whatever it takes but make sure you are replaying them in your mind daily.

3. Exercise one of the following prayers while expecting your deliverance

· 3 day Night Vigil at the Sanctuary (i.e. praying and confessing the Word from 10 pm to 5 am for 3 nights in a row)

· 3 Day Fast (i.e. praying, fasting, and confessing the Word daily from 6 am to 6 pm for 3 days. Alternatively you can fast straight through the 3 days only breaking for communion)

· 3-Day Fasting & Prayer Vigil at the Sanctuary (i.e. praying, fasting, and confessing the Word daily from 10 am to 6 pm for 3 days. Again you can fast continually for 3 days apart from communion)

· 3+ Days Dry Fast (i.e. praying, fasting, and confessing the Word for 3 or more days without taking food or drink). Please note: This should only be done under pastoral recommendation.

4. Pray aggressively while believing that you receive your deliverance

Hebrews 11:6 says, *"We must believe that He is and that He is a rewarder of them that diligently seek Him".*

5. Make any adjustments in your life and repent as the Holy Spirit leads

You have to make sure that you are not leaving any open doors for the enemy to regain access in your life.

6. This is the most crucial step. You must sow your seed to seal your deliverance

Most people sow consecutive seeds, giving it the same name according to their expectation from God regarding their deliverance. To truly succeed in spiritual warfare you have to be a sower. The Bible says in Deuteronomy 16:16 to "never appear before God empty handed". So as you are expecting to receive something from God you need to be giving back something to Him as well.

7. Lastly, prepare yourself for your miracle physically and spiritually

Be vigorous in attending service as much as possible in order to receive the ministration of the Word and the laying on of the hands by the man of God. Also, attend your deliverance sessions regularly if you have been assigned to a mentor.

Bishop Climate Ministries
P.O. Box 67884, London, SE5 9JJ
England, United Kingdom
Tel: +44 7984 115900
Email: partners@bishopclimate.org

Yes Bishop! ENOUGH IS ENOUGH! I want to come into agreement with you that as I sow my seed of Deliverance of £102 according to Psalms 102 I believe that God is going to cancel every demonic appointment with death and failure in my life!

£ _____

Please also send me: Anointed Oil for Total Victory

Here is my Prayer request covering the 7 areas I desire the Lord to manifest His Miracles in my life:

_____

_____

_____

_____

_____

_____

(Continued on Back)

Name:

_____

Address:

_____

_____

_____

Telephone:

_____

Email:

_____

NOTE: You can also sow your special seed SAFELY
& SECURELY online via www.bishopclimate.org

Bishop Climate Ministries is the Healing & Deliverance Ministry founded by Bishop Climate under the anointing and direction of the Holy Spirit. God has anointed Bishop Climate with incredible power to set the captives free. Many people who were unable to get deliverance anywhere else find their freedom as they attend special deliverance sessions conducted through this ministry. The vision of Bishop Climate Ministries is to reach over 1 billion people with the message of deliverance and prosperity, especially in understanding the things of the spirit. Many people are bound because of lack of knowledge and one of the goals of this ministry is to set people free through education.

Child of God I want you to know how much I appreciate you and how special you are to me.

That is why God keeps giving me the wisdom to write these books at such a time as this. He sees your heart and wants you to experience the abundant life that Jesus died for. And so do I. Your support for our ministry is crucial and I hope that you will always continue to lift us up in prayer to God.

I want to take this opportunity to encourage you to partner with us at Bishop Climate Ministries. Hundreds have testified of the miracles that have taken place in their life just as a result of sowing into this ministry and I want you to be able to experience that 100 fold return Jesus spoke about regarding sowing seed into good ground. The Bible says in Proverbs 11:24 *"One person gives freely, yet gains even more; another withholds unduly, but comes to poverty".* Your prayers and financial support are crucial to take this message of salvation and deliverance around the world. And as you do that you can be sure that God is going to bless you beyond your wildest imaginations. There is a 4-fold anointing that you step under when you become a partner with Bishop Climate Ministries. It is the anointing that God has put over my life and this ministry according to Isaiah 11:2. That is the anointing of Divine Direction, Divine Connections, Divine Provision and Divine Protection.

Please understand how much I value you. Your support for our ministry is so crucial and your prayers are as a pillar to us. Your partnership with this ministry is so important and that's why we are committed to praying for you daily and lifting your needs up before God. When you send in your donation please send me a prayer request as well so I can intercede on your behalf before God. I look forward to seeing you in person at our Healing and Deliverance Centre in London, England or at one of our Healing and Deliverance Miracle Crusades.

Remember this is the Ministry where the captives are set free and souls are refreshed.

Remain blessed,

Bishop Climate Irungu

Victory Over The Spirit Of Humiliation & Oppression

Breaking The Curse Of

Good Beginnings & Bad Endings

Victory Over Demonic Assignments

Overcoming Every Generational Hatred

Overcoming Persistent Enemies

Destroying Every Demonic Blockage

Victory Over Every Troubling Spirit

Destroying Every Spirit of Poverty & Lack

Destroying Every Demonic Covenant Over Your Life

Binding the Strongman

Victory Over Every Evil Wish

Breaking Every Demonic Spell

Overturning Every Demonic Judgement

Breaking Every Frustrating Spirit

Destroying Every Demonic Altar

Uprooting Every Territorial Sorcerers

Victory Over Demonic Storms (Marine Spirit)

Bringing Down Goliath (Spirit of Fear)
Dealing With the Spirit of Disappointment
Victory Over The Lying Spirit
Casting Out The Spirit of Anger
Breaking The Spirit Of Pride
Destroying Every Demonic Contamination
Burning Every Spirit Of Mockery

Order Enquiries: Please call our offices or order online at www.bishopclimate.me

24003607R00026

Printed in Great Britain
by Amazon